Disney

FROZEN

make it
Paper Dresses

studio fun BOOKS

White Plains, New York • Montréal, Québec • Bath, United Kingdom

Contents

Be creative! Be a princess!

What you'll find in this book:
- Paper to create Elsa's icy gown
- Ruler
- Stencils for decorations
- Stickers
- 4 paper dresses for your 9-inch fashion dolls, ready to cut out.

What else do you need?
- Assorted colored paper per instructions
- Scissors
- Clear tape (lots of it!)
- Pencil
- Colored pencils, crayons, or markers

Work space
Choose a large table or clear floor space where you can work comfortably. As you finish parts of your gown, you'll need to move them out of the way, so you want to be able to spread out.

Paper
In this book, you'll find all the paper you need to create Elsa's icy gown (plus all four of the dresses for your favorite 9-inch dolls). To make the other dresses, you'll need 9" x 12" colored paper. You can use construction paper or letter-size copier paper—or any other paper of a similar weight and size. Each set of instructions includes guidelines about how many pieces and what colors you need to make each gown, but don't worry if you can't match the colors exactly. You're making your own *Frozen* gowns—be creative and use your imagination to make fantastic dresses!

TIP: Don't use really stiff paper or card stock to make your dresses—you'll end up with a very stiff gown!

Measuring

Use the included ruler to make the measurements described in the instructions. Use a pencil to make small guide marks on the inside of the dress.

Decorating

This is where you can really have a lot of fun. There are special stencils and stickers included to recreate details of Elsa's and Anna's dresses. You can also use markers or crayons or any other shiny, colorful material you can think of. Doilies can give the look of lace to any *Frozen* gown, and wrapping paper, fabric pieces, or glitter can dress up capes and cloaks. Let your imagination run wild and make the fanciest *Frozen* gown ever!

TIP: Decorate your dress before you put it on. It's easier to stick on your fabulous ornaments when the dress is still on a flat work surface.

Taping

You'll need lots of clear tape to make your *Frozen* gowns. Ordinary tape will do, but clear packing tape will make stronger seams. The diagrams suggest where you should place your tape.

Use lots of tape on the inside of the dresses—you might even want to use a few small pieces to reinforce your seams on the outside once the dress is complete.

TIP: Don't worry if a piece of paper rips as you're putting your dress together—just tape it up!

Take a picture!

Modeling your paper dresses

Before you put on your gown, choose clothes to wear underneath. A tank top or undershirt and leggings or a skirt will work well. Think about colors and patterns that match your new *Frozen* gowns.

Take plenty of pictures once your dress is complete. Pop your best pose and save the moment with a photo! Invite your friends over to make dresses together and have a *Frozen* Pose Party!

Elsa's Icy Gown

Now you can relive the magical moment when Elsa creates her beautiful crystal-blue gown. Follow these simple steps to create your very own gown and cape!

pattern A

pattern B

pattern C

TOP

Paper needed: 3 sheets, pattern A

1. Fold one sheet of paper in half, short sides together, as shown. Open it up again and cut along the fold.

2. Take the other two sheets of paper and place them together. Measure 4 inches from the top of the sheets and make a mark with your pencil. Then measure 3 inches from the bottom and mark with your pencil.

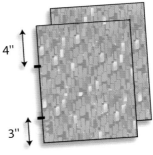

4"

3"

3. Fold both sheets of paper together from the corners to the spots you have marked, as shown.

TIP: This is a tricky fold. You can use your ruler to draw a line from the upper right corner to your mark and fold along that line. Or try placing your ruler along the line you want to fold, and use it to guide your fold.

4. Measure 3 inches from the top corner on both sides and draw a line across with your pencil. Cut the folded corner off along the line.

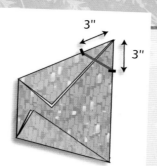

5. Separate the two sheets of paper. Reverse the folds on one piece. Line up all the pieces as shown and tape them together. Fold the outer pieces of paper to align with the top. The taped side will be the inside of your top.

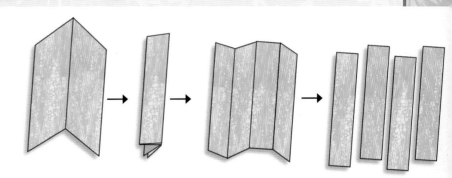

SKIRT

Paper needed: 13 sheets, pattern B

1. Fold one sheet of paper in half, long sides together. Fold it in half again, as shown. Unfold and cut along the folds.

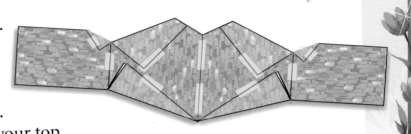

2. Line the pieces up so they overlap by around ½ inch at the top only, as shown, and tape them together. Notice how the belt curves a bit.

3. Place five sheets of paper on top of the belt, in the order shown. Overlap the side edges about 2 inches at the top to follow the curve of the belt. Tape the sheets.

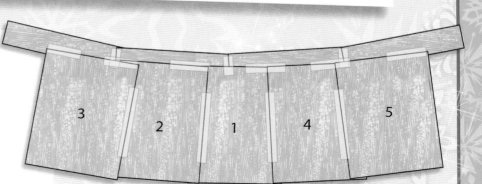

4. Create a second row the same way with five more sheets of paper. Tape the sheets as shown.

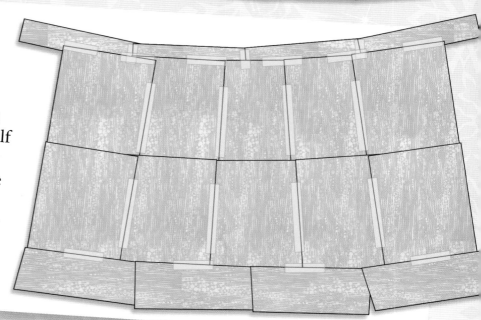

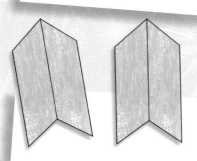

5. Fold two sheets of paper in half so the long sides meet, and cut in half on your fold lines. Use these four pieces to make the bottom row of your skirt. Use tape only along the top edge of this row. Your skirt is done!

CAPE

Paper needed: 14 sheets, pattern C

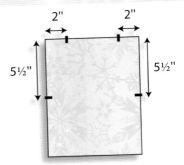

1. Make four marks on the edges of one sheet of paper as shown.

2. Line up two more sheets of paper, one on either side, with the top corners at the top pencil marks and the sides meeting at the lower pencil marks.

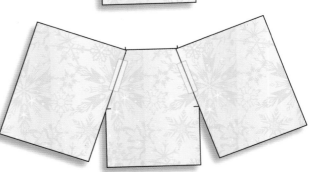

3. Tape on two more sheets as shown, overlapping by an inch or so.

4. Fold one piece of paper so the two short ends meet. Then fold it again, as shown. Unfold it and cut along the fold marks.

5. Tape two pieces end to end, then do the same with the other two pieces.

6. Line up the two taped sections as shown. Tape onto the cape.

7. Tape three more sheets of paper at the bottom, overlapping by about an inch.

8. Stack two sheets together and fold one corner down so the edges meet at the opposite side. Trim off the bottom. Unfold and cut along the diagonal so you have four triangles.

9. Tape two triangles on the left and right sides as shown.

10. Tape one more sheet of paper to the middle.

11. Tape two triangles on the left and right, connecting to the middle.

12. Tape the last two sheets of paper as shown.

Have fun decorating your gown! You'll find some snowflake stickers and a snowflake press-out in this book—you can even use the press-out as a stencil to make more snowflakes. Add some silvery, sparkling dots cut out of foil or sparkly paper, or even stick-on jewels, to add a shimmery look to your dress and cape.

Add big snowflakes for decoration. Turn the page to learn how to make them!

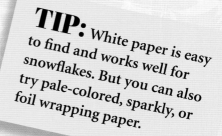

SNOWFLAKES

Paper needed: white
(1 sheet makes 1 snowflake);
stencil #1

TIP: White paper is easy to find and works well for snowflakes. But you can also try pale-colored, sparkly, or foil wrapping paper.

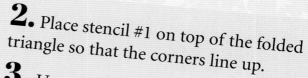

1. Fold one corner down so the edges meet at the opposite side. Trim off the bottom.

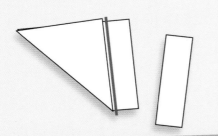

2. Place stencil #1 on top of the folded triangle so that the corners line up.

3. Use a pencil to trace around the outside and inside shapes.

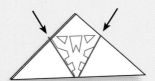

4. Use your ruler to draw lines, as shown, then fold along the lines.

5. Cut off the top area, using the top edges of the outlined shapes as a guide.

6. Cut out the outlined shapes, then carefully unfold to reveal your snowflake! Repeat for as many snowflakes as you want.

Dress up in your gown!

Now you're ready to put on your icy gown. Here's how to do it!

1. Start with your skirt. Wrap it around your waist to fit snugly but comfortably.

TIP: Choose what you're going to be wearing underneath. For this gown, a white or blue undershirt and leggings or a skirt would be great.

2. Attach the waistband securely with tape. If you need to, adjust the length by folding the bottom up or even trimming it.

3. Put on the top, attaching it in back with tape.

4. Now put on the cape. Overlap the straps in a V shape in the front, attaching them with tape or paperclips. Princess Elsa is ready!

Take a picture!

TIP: If you want to save your dress for another day, ask an adult to cut the tape with a scissors to remove the skirt and top.

Anna's Blue Dress

Wearing this cozy and colorful winter outfit, Anna rode through the wilderness to rescue her sister. Now you can make Anna's beautiful outfit, too!

9 sheets dark blue

4 sheets light blue

stickers to use

SKIRT

What you need: 9 sheets of medium or dark blue paper, 4 sheets of light blue paper, stencil #2, stickers

stencil #2

1. Fold a sheet of the darker paper in half, long sides together. Place stencil #2 at the bottom as shown. Trace around the curve, then trace the inside the holes. Repeat on the other side.

2. Cut along the outside curve.

3. Repeat steps 1 and 2 with three more sheets of paper.

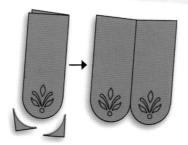

4. Find the matching sticker shapes and stick them on the paper, using your pencil outlines as a guide.

5. Fold one sheet of paper in half, long sides together. Fold it in half again, as shown. Unfold and cut along the folds.

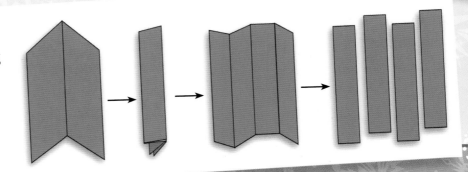

6. Line the pieces up so they overlap by around ½ inch at the top only, as shown, and tape them together to make a curved belt.

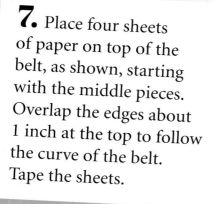

7. Place four sheets of paper on top of the belt, as shown, starting with the middle pieces. Overlap the edges about 1 inch at the top to follow the curve of the belt. Tape the sheets.

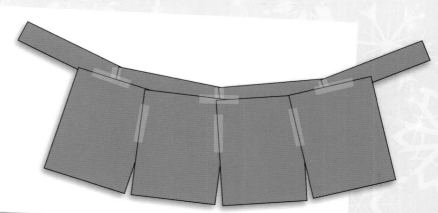

8. Tape on a second row with four sheets of the lighter blue paper, placing them the long way.

9. Layer the decorated pieces over the top of the skirt on the front. Tape them along the top edge only.

10. Put on the other stickers, as shown. Your skirt is done!

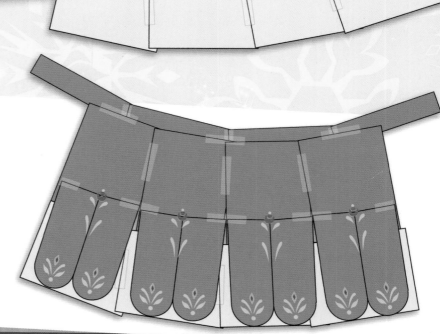
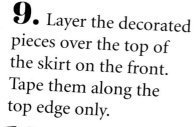

TOP

What you need:

3 sheets of black paper, stickers, stencils #3 and #4

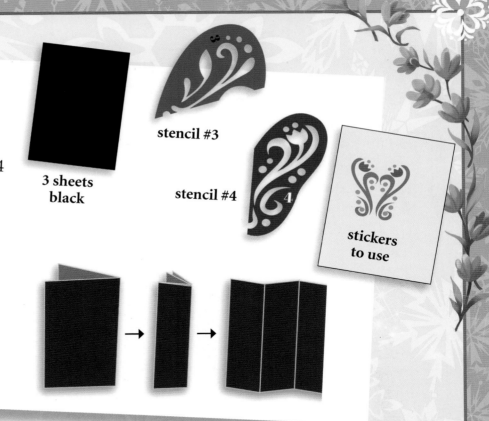

3 sheets black

stencil #3

stencil #4

stickers to use

1. Fold one sheet of paper so the two short ends meet. Then fold it again, as shown (this will create guidelines for the next steps). Unfold once, so paper is folded in half, with the folded edge on your right.

TIP: If it is hard to see your pencil marks on the black paper, try using a white or yellow colored pencil.

2. Use your ruler to measure and mark 1½ inches from the top left, and 2½ inches from the top right. Also mark 2 inches up from the bottom on the left side, and make a mark at the center fold line on the bottom edge, as shown.

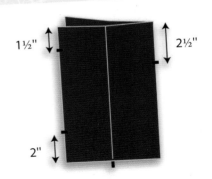

1½" 2½" 2"

3. Use a pencil and stencil #3 to draw a curved line, as shown. Make another curved line on the bottom left corner, as shown, using the top of the stencil. Cut along the curved lines.

4. Unfold the paper and throw away the scraps from the bottom cuts. Cut the top piece along the left and right fold lines. Throw away the two small pieces and keep the pointed center piece. Tape this piece to the bottom of your larger piece, as shown. You'll have a heart shape!

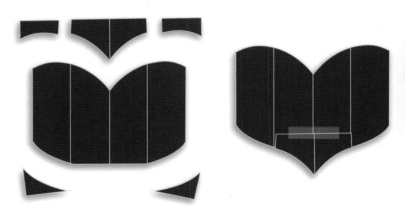

5. Fold another sheet of paper in half, short sides together. Unfold and cut along the fold.

6. Tape a piece on either side of the heart shape.

7. On another sheet of paper, use your ruler to mark 2 inches from the top on the left side, and 2 inches from the bottom on the right side, as shown. Draw a line between the marks. Cut along the line to make two pieces.

2"

2"

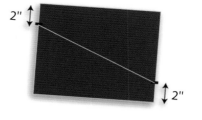

8. Make marks around the middle of each short side (they don't have to be exact). Draw a line between the marks, then fold each piece along this line. Reverse the fold on one piece. These will be the shoulder straps for your top.

9. Tape the smaller ends of the straps to the top of the heart shape. Keep the folded edges facing each other. Your top is ready for decoration!

10. Put stencil #4 on one side along the center fold line, then use your pencil to trace around the inside shapes. Flip the stencil over and do the same on the other side.

11. Find and stick on the matching stickers, putting them over the pencil lines.

TIP: Have you used your stickers already? That's fine—just make your own decoration using pretty colored paper!

CAPE

What you need:

8 sheets of pink paper, stencil #2

8 sheets pink

stencil #2

1. Fold one sheet of paper in half so the short sides meet, then unfold it. This fold mark will be a guideline.

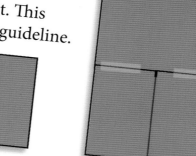

2. Tape the folded piece to another sheet of paper, matching the long sides.

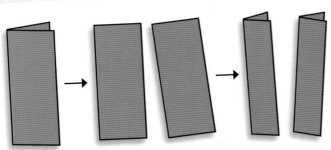

3. Fold a sheet of paper in half so the long sides meet. Unfold and cut along the fold line.

4. Fold these smaller pieces of paper in half so the long sides meet.

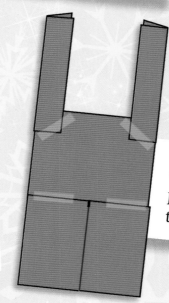

5. Tape these pieces to the top of the cape, as shown.

6. Fold two sheet of paper so the long sides meet. Place your stencil at one end, as shown, and trace around the curves. Cut out the curved shape, then cut this in half along the fold line. Repeat on the second sheet.

7. Attach the pieces with the curved ends to two more sheets of paper as shown.

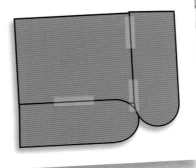

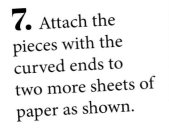

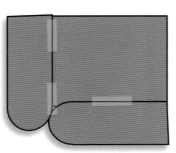

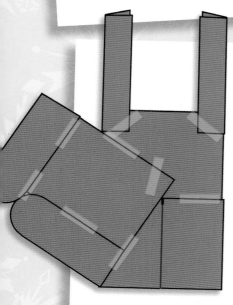

8. Take one of the pieces you just made and attach it so the bottom corners of both pieces line up. Tape securely, then attach the second piece on the other side in the same way.

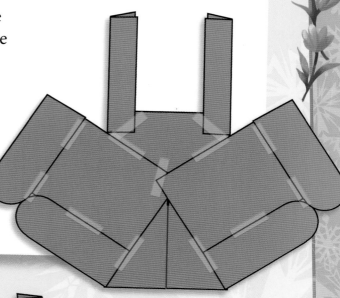

9. Using your stencil, trace and cut two corners from another sheet of paper.

TIP: Before you put your cape on, you can decorate it with a traditional scalloped design just like Anna's. Use a glass or a mug to mark a border of semicircles all around the cape, then use a purple or blue marker to color in the edge.

10. Attach this piece to the bottom of your cape, as shown. Your pink cape is ready!

Dress up in your gown!

Now you're ready to put on your dress! Here's how to do it!

1. Start with the skirt, wrapping it around your waist to fit snugly but comfortably. Attach the waistband securely with tape.

2. Put on the top, attaching it in the back with tape.

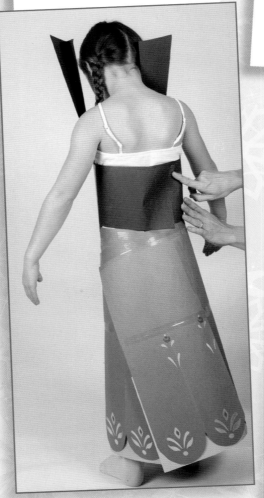

3. Bring the straps over the shoulders and secure them with tape in the back. You're almost ready to rescue Elsa!

4. Put on the cape, bringing the straps around to the front, overlapping them and securing them to the cape as shown. Anna to the rescue!

Take a picture!

Elsa's Royal Gown

Wearing the gown Elsa wore to be crowned queen, you'll be as royal as she is in your own version of this dress!

SKIRT

What you need:
13 sheets of teal paper, stencil #5

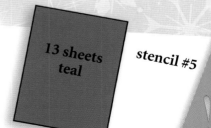

13 sheets teal   stencil #5

1. Fold two sheets of paper so the short sides meet, then cut these in half along the fold line. Use your ruler to measure 2 inches in on the long side, as shown.

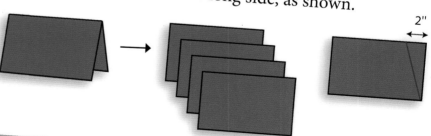

2"

2. Line up the four pieces so they meet at the bottom corners but overlap to the mark you made at the top, as shown.

3. Fold three sheets of paper so the long ends meet, then cut them on the fold lines. You'll need these pieces starting with step 5.

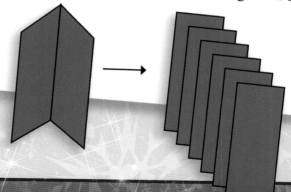

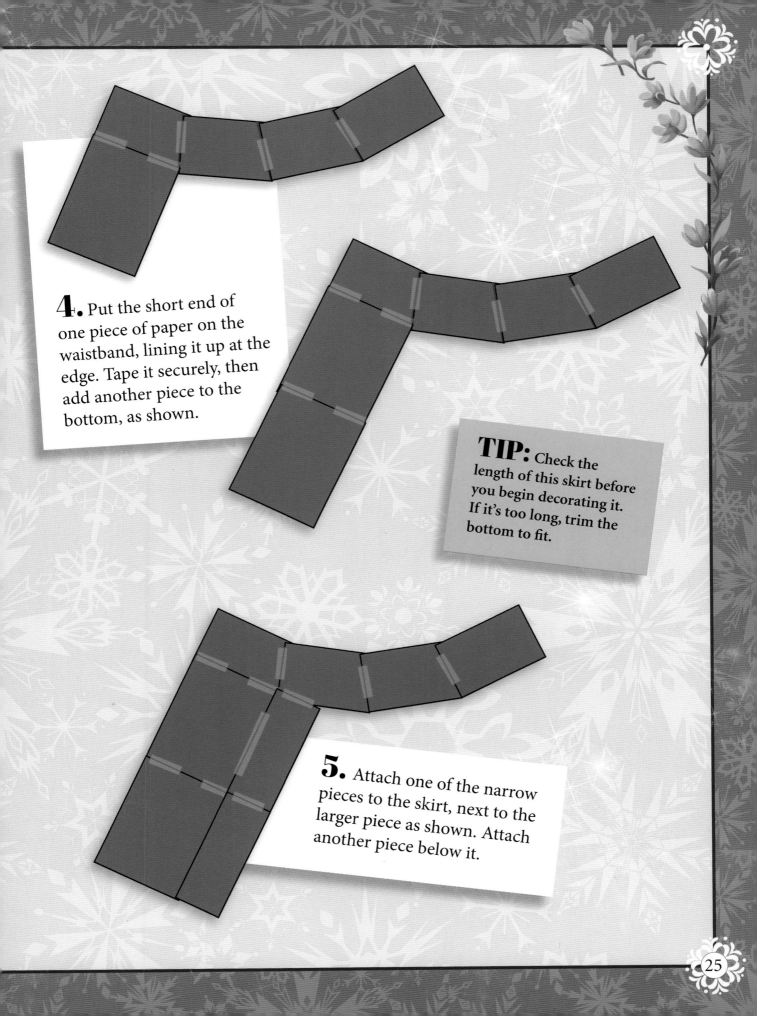

4. Put the short end of one piece of paper on the waistband, lining it up at the edge. Tape it securely, then add another piece to the bottom, as shown.

TIP: Check the length of this skirt before you begin decorating it. If it's too long, trim the bottom to fit.

5. Attach one of the narrow pieces to the skirt, next to the larger piece as shown. Attach another piece below it.

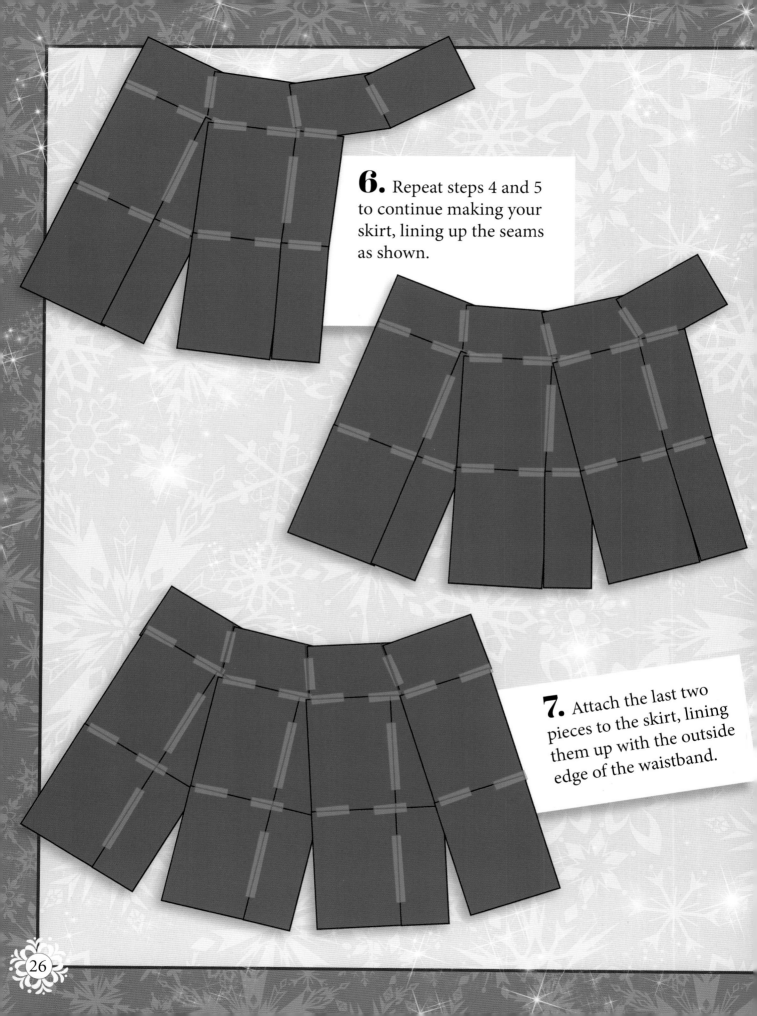

6. Repeat steps 4 and 5 to continue making your skirt, lining up the seams as shown.

7. Attach the last two pieces to the skirt, lining them up with the outside edge of the waistband.

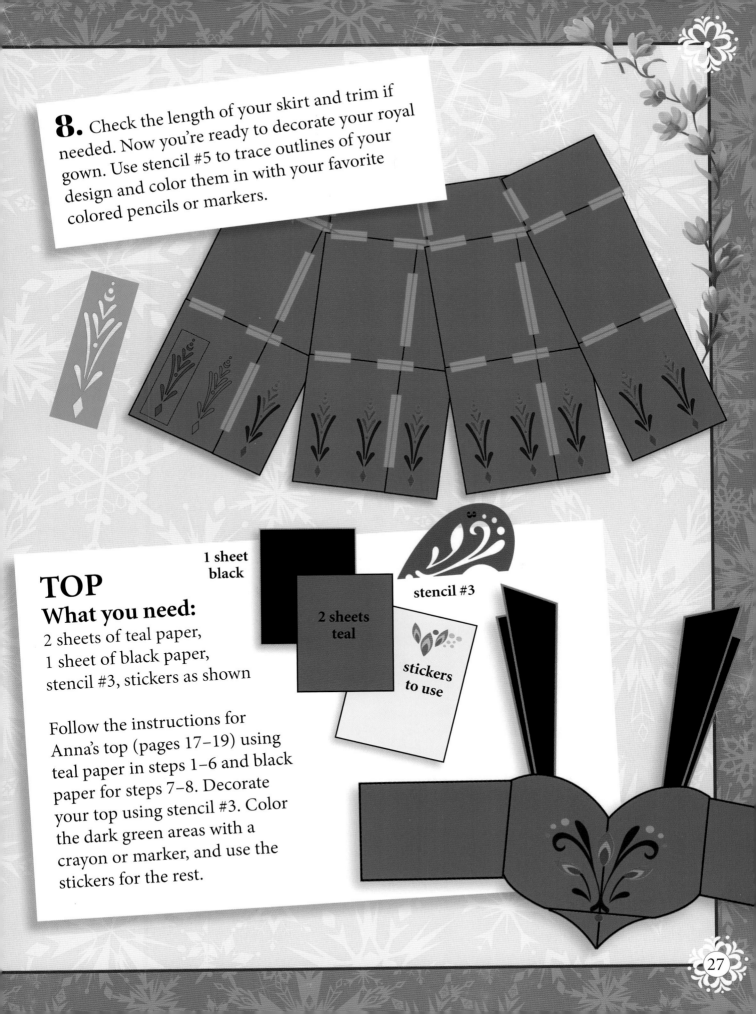

8. Check the length of your skirt and trim if needed. Now you're ready to decorate your royal gown. Use stencil #5 to trace outlines of your design and color them in with your favorite colored pencils or markers.

1 sheet black

2 sheets teal

stencil #3

stickers to use

TOP
What you need:
2 sheets of teal paper,
1 sheet of black paper,
stencil #3, stickers as shown

Follow the instructions for Anna's top (pages 17–19) using teal paper in steps 1–6 and black paper for steps 7–8. Decorate your top using stencil #3. Color the dark green areas with a crayon or marker, and use the stickers for the rest.

CAPE

What you need:
14 sheets of purple or dark pink paper

14 sheets purple

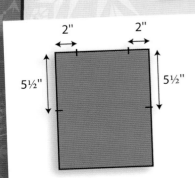

1. On one sheet of paper, use your ruler to mark 2 inches in from each side on the short side, and 5½ inches down on each long side, as shown.

2. Use your pencil marks as guides to attach two more sheets of paper, one on each side, as shown.

3. Tape on two more sheets as shown, overlapping at the top.

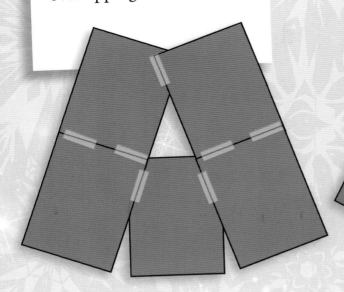

4. Add two more sheets at the bottom, placing them the long way and lining them up on the outside edge.

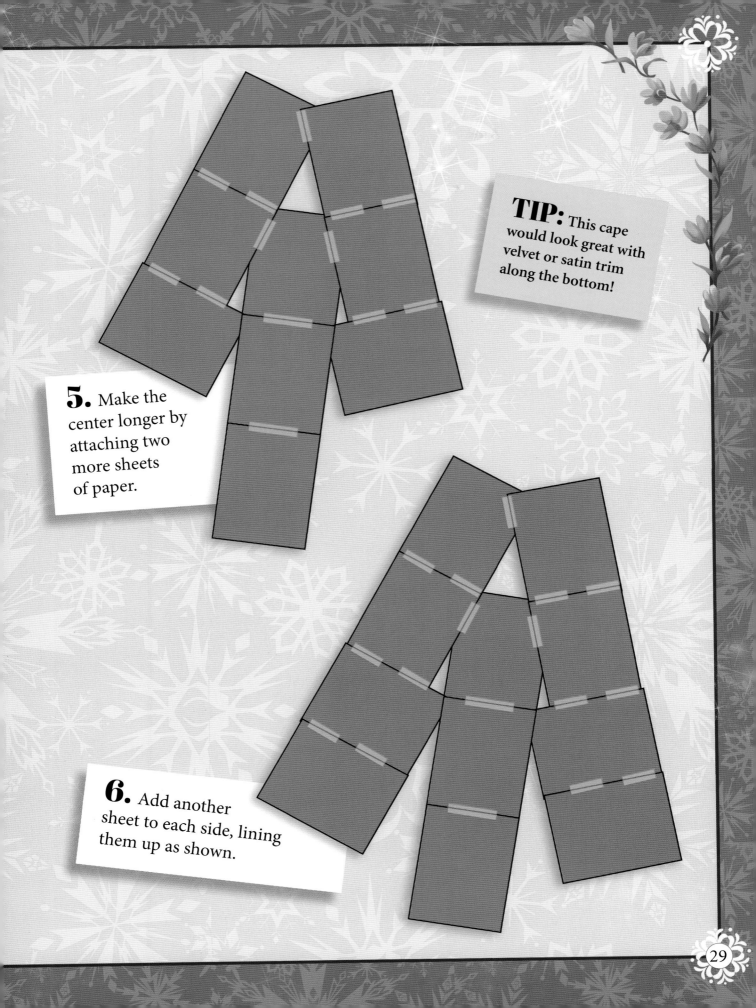

TIP: This cape would look great with velvet or satin trim along the bottom!

5. Make the center longer by attaching two more sheets of paper.

6. Add another sheet to each side, lining them up as shown.

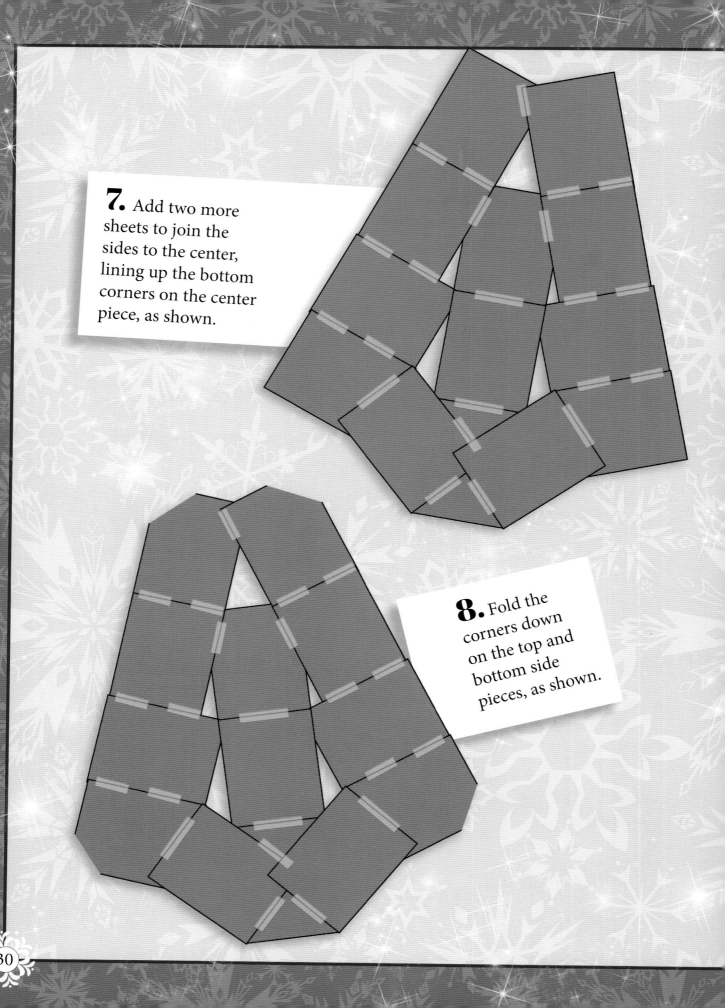

7. Add two more sheets to join the sides to the center, lining up the bottom corners on the center piece, as shown.

8. Fold the corners down on the top and bottom side pieces, as shown.

9. With another sheet of paper, fold one corner down so the edges meet at the opposite side. Trim off the bottom, then unfold and cut along the diagonal so you have two triangles.

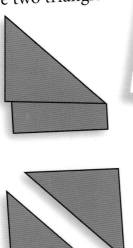

10. Attach these triangles to the top of the cape so you have a large collar. Your cape is done!

CROWN

Press out the crown from the stencil page, and fold it along the green lines. With a small piece of tape, attach the two pieces of the base together, as shown. Use bobby pins through the small holes to keep it on your head.

Dress up in your gown!

1. Start with the skirt, wrapping it around your waist to fit snugly but comfortably. Attach the waistband securely with tape.

2. Put on the top, attaching it with tape in the back.

3. Bring the straps over the shoulders and secure them with tape in the back.

JEWEL

Press out the jewel from the stencil page, and tape it to the cape at the neck.

5. With your crown and your jewel at your neck, you're a very royal princess!

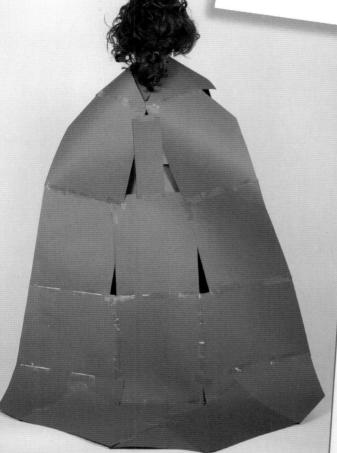

4. Put on the cape, attaching it in front at the neckline.

Take a picture!

Anna's Green Dress

In the beautiful dress she wore for her sister's coronation, Anna looked like a perfect princess—and so will you!

SKIRT
What you need:
8 sheets of light green paper,
6 sheets of dark green paper,
stencil #6

stencil #6

8 sheets
light green

6 sheets dark green

1. Start by folding six sheets of light green paper in half the long way, then cutting along the fold line. Do the same with six sheets of dark green paper. Now you have 12 pieces of light green paper and 12 pieces of dark green paper. Tape two pieces of light green paper together to make a long strip, and do the same with two pieces of dark green paper.

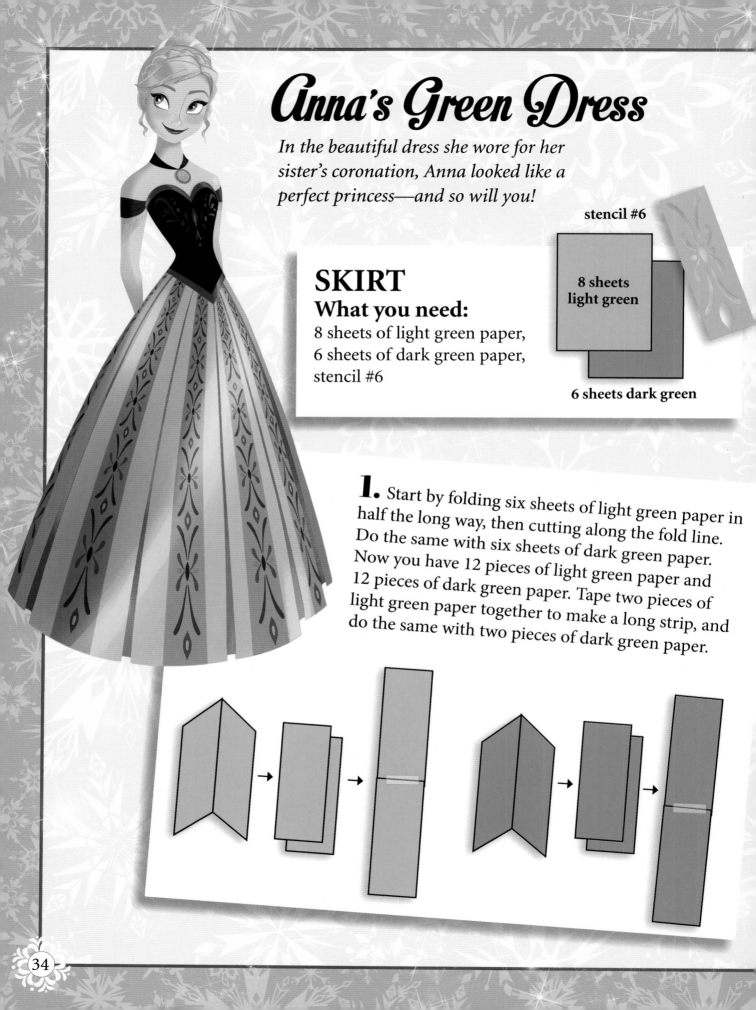

2. Line up the strips next to each other and tape them together, at the top only, as shown. Repeat with the remaining paper, ending up with six striped pieces.

3. Now you can begin joining them. Line up one piece against the other, light green next to dark green. At the top, the light green pieces should touch, as shown, and at the bottom, the light green piece should meet at the outer edge of the dark green piece.

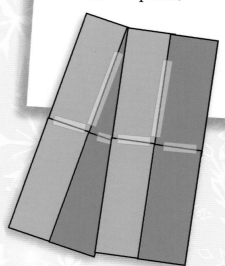

4. Tape these sections together. Repeat, using all your panels, until you have a striped skirt.

5. Fold two sheets of light green paper so the short sides meet. Unfold and cut along the fold lines.

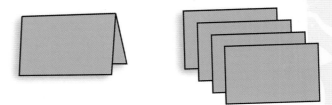

6. You'll use these four pieces to make a waistband for your skirt. Hold the striped skirt up to see how long it is. You can adjust the length depending on where you attach the waistband pieces. Tape on one waistband piece, lining it up with the outer edge of the skirt.

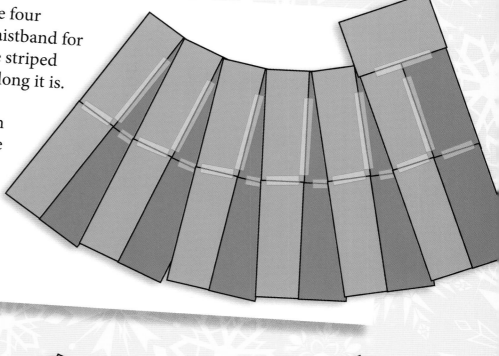

7. Continue taping on the waistband pieces, lining them up along the top.

8. Now it's time to decorate your skirt. Use stencil #6 to mark the pattern on the dark green pieces of paper, and color them in, using markers or colored pencils. Your skirt is done!

TOP
What you need:
3 sheets of black paper, stencil #7, stickers as shown

Follow the instructions for Anna's top (pages 17–19). Decorate your top using stencil #7 and the stickers.

3 sheets black

stickers to use

stencil #7

Dress up in your gown!

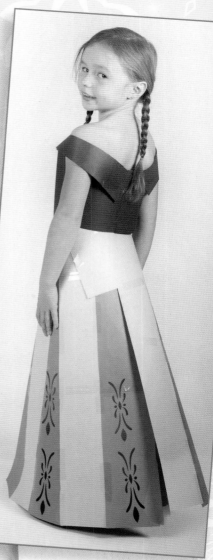

1. Start with the skirt, wrapping it around your waist to fit snugly but comfortably. Attach the waistband securely with tape.

2. Put on the top, attaching it with tape in the back. Fold the shoulder straps over in the front, as shown, to create an off-the-shoulder look.

3. Attach the shoulder straps in the back with tape.

JEWEL

For Anna's necklace, cut out the black straps on the page with your doll's top, or use black paper of your own. Press out the green jewel—it's on the stencil page.

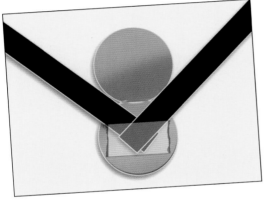

Tape the straps on one side of the inside of the jewel, as shown, and fold the top over.

To wear your necklace, either tape or twist the straps together.

 **Take a picture!**

4. With your jeweled necklace, you're ready for the Coronation Ball!

Dress up your dolls!

You can dress up your favorite 9-inch dolls in Frozen gowns so they can join the party, too!

ELSA'S ICY GOWN

1. Carefully tear out the pages with Elsa's icy gown and cape.

2. Fold the pages in half along the center line.

3. Cut out the dress and the cape along the black lines. Cut along the lines on the bottom of the skirt.

4. Wrap the skirt around your doll's waist and tape.

5. Fold the front neckline area of the top down as shown. Wrap the top around your doll, and tape it in the back.

6. Fasten the cape by wrapping the straps around the doll's arms, as shown, and taping them down.

ANNA'S BLUE DRESS

1. Carefully tear out the pages with Anna's blue dress and cape.

2. Fold the pages in half along the center line.

3. Cut out the dress and the cape along the yellow lines.

4. Wrap the skirt around your doll's waist and tape.

5. Wrap the top around your doll, and tape in the back.

6. Tape the cape in front, as shown.

ELSA'S ROYAL GOWN

1. Carefully tear out the pages with Elsa's royal gown and cape.

2. Fold the pages in half along the center line.

3. Cut out the dress and cape along the pink lines, cutting along the lines on the bottom of the skirt as well.

4. Wrap the dress around your doll and tape in the back. Slide the bottom strap under her arms and keep the top strap over her shoulders.

5. Attach the top strap to the skirt in the back, as shown, and wrap the bottom strap around her arms.

6. Fasten the cape in front, as shown.

ANNA'S GREEN DRESS

1. Carefully tear out the pages with Anna's green skirt and top.

2. Fold the pages in half along the center lines.

3. Cut out the dress and the top along the blue lines.

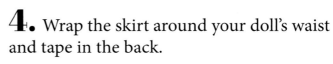

4. Wrap the skirt around your doll's waist and tape in the back.

5. Wrap the top around your doll and tape in the back. Wrap the straps around to the back and tape as shown.

**ELSA'S ICY
GOWN**
for your doll
(see instructions
on page 40)

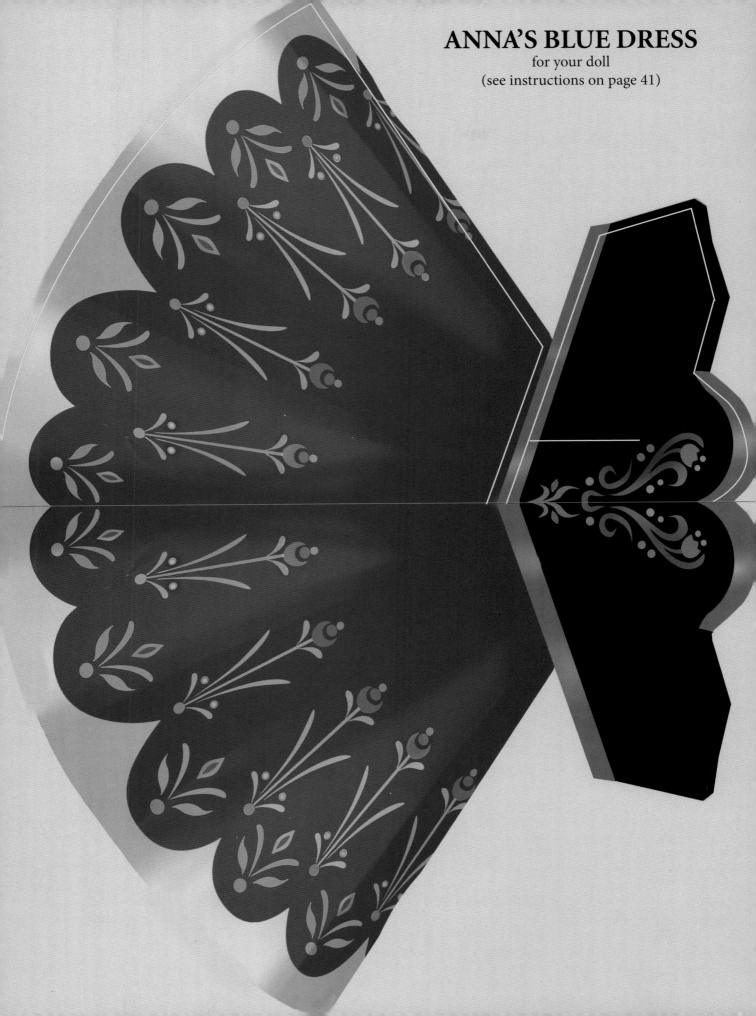

ANNA'S BLUE DRESS
for your doll
(see instructions on page 41)

ANNA'S BLUE DRESS
for your doll
(see instructions on page 41)

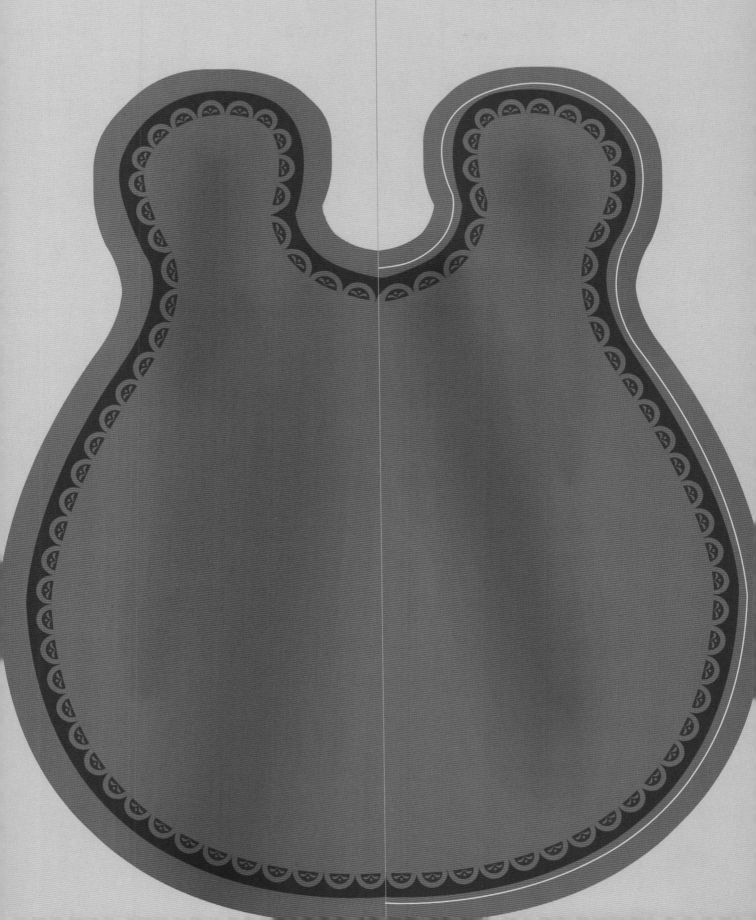

ELSA'S ROYAL GOWN
for your doll
(see instructions on page 42)

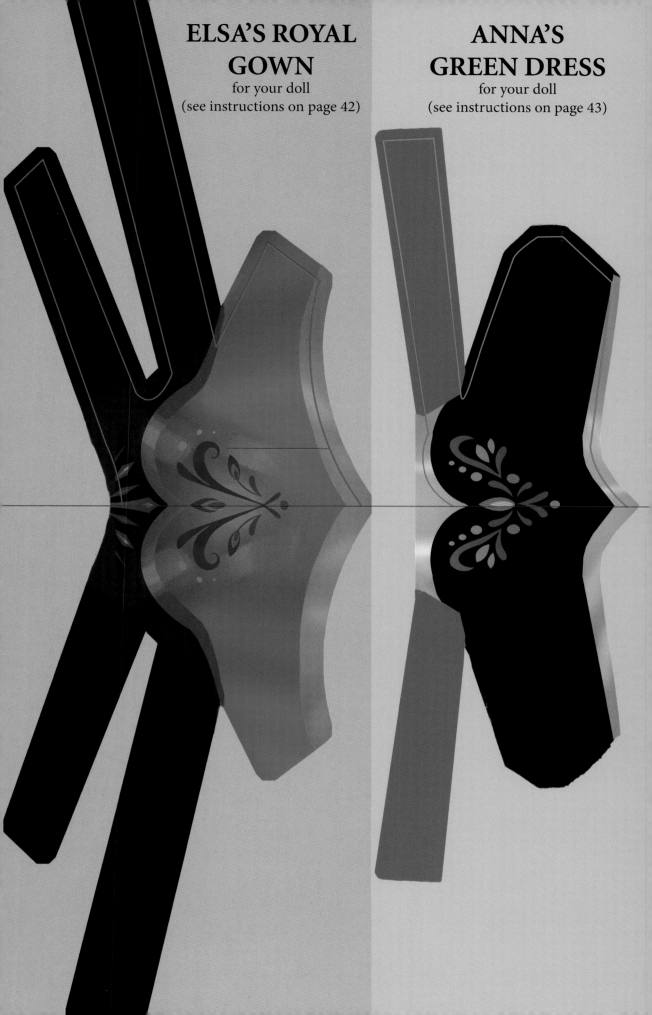

ELSA'S ROYAL GOWN
for your doll
(see instructions on page 42)

ANNA'S GREEN DRESS
for your doll
(see instructions on page 43)

ELSA'S ROYAL GOWN
for your doll
(see instructions on page 42)

ANNA'S
GREEN DRESS
for your doll
(see instructions on page 43)

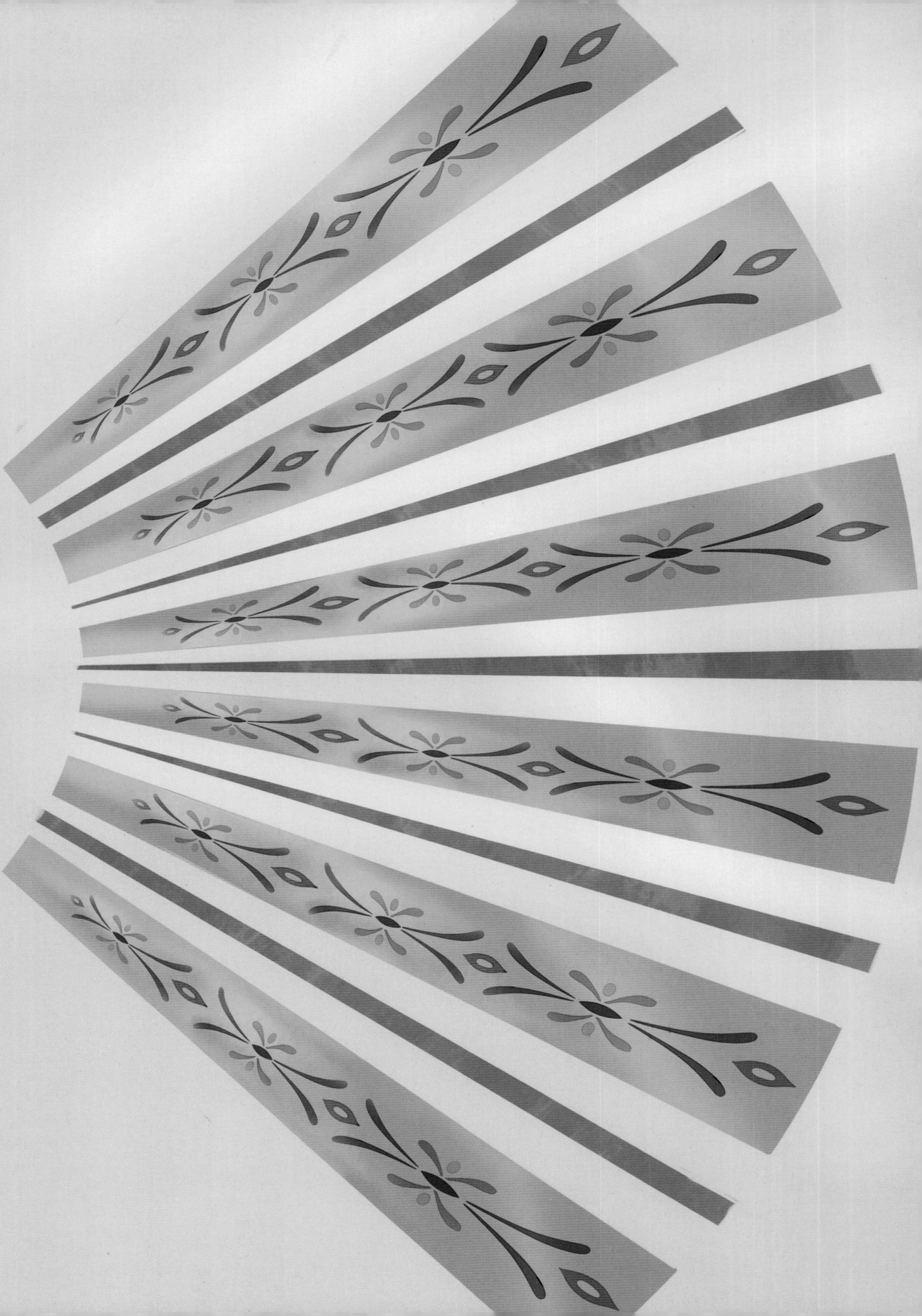

Warning! Keep away from fire.

Warning! Keep away from fire.

Warning! Keep away from fire.

Warning! Keep away from fire.

Warning! Keep away from fire.

Warning! Keep away from fire.

Warning! Keep away from fire.

Warning! Keep away from fire.

Warning! Keep away from fire.

Warning! Keep away from fire.

Warning! Keep away from fire.

Warning! Keep away from fire.

Warning! Keep away from fire.

Warning! Keep away from fire.

Warning! Keep away from fire.

Warning! Keep away from fire.

Warning! Keep away from fire.